CHICKAREE
A Red Squirrel

CHICKAREE
A Red Squirrel

Written and illustrated

by St. Tamara

Harcourt Brace Jovanovich   New York and London

To my father

Requests for permission to make copies of any part of the work should be mailed to:
Permissions, Harcourt Brace Jovanovich, Inc., 757 Third Avenue, New York, New York
10017
Printed in the United States of America

Library of Congress Cataloging in Publication Data

St. Tamara.
Chickaree, a red squirrel.
Summary: Describes a year in the life
of a red squirrel as she mates twice
and brings up two sets of babies.
1. Tamiasciurus hudsonicus—Juvenile literature.
[1. Red squirrels. 2. Squirrels.] I. Title.
QL737.R68S28   1980   599'.3232   79-23933
ISBN 0-15-216612-2

First edition

B C D E

HBJ

Chickaree is not sleepy.

She sits on the branch near her nest and listens. Her curled paws pressed to her body keep her naked, pink thumbs from freezing. The rest of her body is covered and warmed by her bushy tail. It is night, and the snow glistens in the moonlight.

Suddenly Chickaree perks up her tufted ears. Down below she sees a dark shadow moving slowly closer to her tree.

"Tsuh-tsuh-tsuh," Chickaree warns the intruder. The dark body below moves away, leaving deep footprints in the snow. It is a fox looking for cottontails.

Chickaree feels thirsty and nibbles on some snow nearby. She must drink water every day, and in winter snow is a substitute. Now she listens for other intruders, but there is only the hooting of an owl, so she returns to her warm nest to sleep.

Chickaree is a red, or pine, squirrel of North America whose Latin name is *Tamiasciurus* (*tamias*, a storer; *sciurus*, shadow of a tail) *hudsonicus*. According to chickarees, she is now mature and independent, that is, about ten months old and ready to choose a mate. She has made her first home in an abandoned flicker's nest in the cavity of an evergreen, which she has lined with moss and dried leaves.

When she awakens at daybreak, she looks over the snow-covered ground of the forest, then quickly and jerkily runs down the tree head-first. On the way she stops to wipe her nose on the bark and to stretch, hanging by the sharp claws of her hind paws. On the ground she hops over the snow haltingly, sniffing for pine cones. Her sense of smell is so well developed that she can find her food caches hidden under several inches of snow. Scratching the snow, she finds a pine cone and holds it in her mouth, twirling it with her paws for inspection. Satisfied, she climbs with the cone in her mouth to her favorite branch to begin her day with breakfast.

Chickaree is busy all day and every day of the year, inspecting her territory, defending it ferociously if need be, chasing pesky gray squirrels, other chickarees, and birds away from her food caches. These caches are scattered all over her territory, which is about one square acre of woods.

In one cache Chickaree has hidden almost one hundred and fifty pine cones. They have been stored green in damp soil to keep them from ripening too fast, opening up and loosing seeds. Each cache is covered with dry leaves and is waterproof. Not all of Chickaree's food is stored in the ground. Nuts and acorns, their green flesh removed to prevent rot, are hidden in an abandoned crow's nest. More are hidden in a dry place under some logs, together with dried mushrooms and other fungi. The mushrooms have been tucked between pine needles to dry. It is easy for Chickaree to inspect her cache of sweet-gum tree cones, for they are hidden around her nest tree trunk well covered with dry leaves.

Several times a day Chickaree sits on her branch and rids herself of parasites: fleas, ticks, mites, and nematodes. First she wipes her nose on the tree bark and then wipes her face with her paws, after wetting them with her tongue. Now she cleans her right paw while holding it with her left; then she cleans her left paw holding it with her right. She licks her sides and gives extra attention to her tail because it is such an important part of her body. It serves as a balance pole, a rudder in an emergency jump, a warm blanket when it is cold, and an umbrella on rainy days. (Male chickarees also use their tails to make signals during courtship.)

The winter days pass at last, and soon Chickaree hears the first call of the spring peeper. Soon the woods become alive with more bird songs and the chatter of other chickarees. It is time for the male chickarees to invade the female territory, and their chatter, squeaks, coos, and growls almost drown the bird songs as the females try to chase away the males. The early spring mating game has begun!

tseew-tseew   kghsee-kghsee

ch-r-r-r-r-r-r-r-r-r-r-r-r-r-r-r

gr-r-r

chr-r-r-r-

tsee-tsee-tsee-chr

In small groups of threes and fours, chickarees spiral up and down the trees. They leap from branch to branch, from tree to tree, chasing each other on the ground. As they run, each makes soft coughing sounds: kghsee-kghsee-kghsee. After a while they disperse, but soon seek each other's company again. The courtship game goes on for days before they pair off.

Chickaree and her male companion have become inseparable. Suddenly, however, a new male chickaree appears, and a fight has begun. Male chickarees fight ferociously to establish supremacy and claim a mate. They box and bite and roll over the ground locked together. They scream and bare their teeth, lunge at each other, break up, then begin anew. The fight continues until the weaker one runs away, as does this stranger at last. The winner and Chickaree then mate, and she invites him to her nest to live.

The following days are busy for Chickaree. Choosing a forked branch high in a pine tree protected by dense foliage, she has begun to build a new nest. Her male companion helps her only a little, and it is all the help she will get from him. Finished, the nest resembles a huge shaggy ball, made from twigs with a few leaves still attached. The inside of her nest Chickaree has lined with shredded bark, dry leaves, moss, and even some fur and feathers she has found. The nest has two holes: entry and exit. The exit hole is kept closed except for emergencies. Not every chickaree has built her nest like this, however. One may have made use of an abandoned hawk's nest, another an empty woodchuck's lair underground.

The buds swell on a nearby maple tree, and
Chickaree eats them hungrily. Now she makes
a cut in a bark, and as the sap swells, Chickaree
drinks it thirstily. Then she leaps to an elm tree
to eat its plump buds. Chickaree is restless. She
darts at a chipmunk who has just awakened
from a long winter's sleep. She feels a need to
be alone. Finally she even chases away her
mate and retreats to her nest.

Five weeks later, four tiny babies are born to Chickaree. Some chickarees may have up to eight babies, but the average is four or five. The babies are hairless, pink, and helpless. Born blind, each is about two inches long. They all have a fold of skin along their sides that will disappear as they grow.

Chickaree picks up one baby in her paws and licks him clean. She turns him over and over, cleaning every part of his tiny body. One by one she thoroughly cleans the other three. Afterward she tucks them against the nipples on her belly and feeds them. The warm milk makes them sleepy. Chickaree covers them with her bushy tail, and soon they all fall asleep.

At dawn Chickaree leaves her sleeping babies and runs up the tree to retrieve a dry mushroom. She eats it quickly and then runs down the tree to get a pine cone from one of her caches. She is busy, but she is also alert and extremely cautious. Now she has found a green patch of moss glistening with morning dew. She wipes her nose, then flops on her belly and slithers over the wet moss again and again. Abruptly she perks up her ears and listens for enemies, then runs up the tree and sits on a branch to groom herself. The spring sun is warm and makes her sleepy. Her eyelids get heavier and heavier, but she dares not close them, for she must watch over her babies.

Y-e-e-ek! screams a blue jay, and Mother

Chickaree freezes for a moment, then quickly disappears inside her nest.

The baby chickarees grow quickly. Within ten days, soft, fluffy hair has grown over their pink skin, and the fold on their sides has disappeared. They gain strength and begin to move around slowly, clumsily. But they are still blind.

Chickaree keeps close watch on her nest. Attracted by the babies' squeaky cries, a huge black crow alights. Chickaree charges at it, and with a startled cry the crow takes flight. Last night she had chased away an owl.

Spring has now burst into full bloom. Bumblebees are collecting nectar from violets and marsh marigolds. Fiddlehead ferns unfurl their heads, trees and bushes stand in a fresh green whisper of new leaves, and the white flowers of the dogwoods tremble in a soft breeze.

The baby chickarees are nineteen days old. Their fluffy hair is gone, and they have grown a new rusty-colored permanent coat. They grow larger and stronger each day and look exactly like their mother. But still they are blind.

As the babies grow, they sleep less and demand more and more of their mother's attention. Chickaree spends most of her time cleaning and nursing them, with little time to doze or bask in the sun, which chickarees love so much to do.

One narrow slit of light appears between the babies' eyelids. Gradually it grows wider, and at last they can see! Since chickarees are curious by nature, keeping them blind for so long is nature's way of keeping the babies out of trouble. Already the babies want to see beyond the light coming through the nest's entry hole. But Chickaree nudges them away. They are not yet ready to face the world outside.

The nest, however, has become too small for her growing family, and Chickaree inspects a large summer nest abandoned by another chickaree only a few pine trees away. The next day she picks up one baby in her mouth and carries it to the summer nest while it beats the air with its tiny paws. She deposits it there and returns to fetch her second baby. Then she transfers her third and fourth babies and returns to the old nest to make sure none are left behind.

Pfe-e-e-e-e-e-e-e!

Chickaree has never heard this whistle before, yet she knows what has happened. A baby has fallen out of the nest! When a baby chickaree falls, he emits a long whistle, a lost signal. Chickaree rushes down the tree trunk to her fallen baby screaming tsee-tsee-tsee-chr! Finding her baby uninjured (chickarees always land on their feet), Chickaree picks him up in her mouth and carries him back up the tree to the nest.

In this new summer nest the babies have room to play. They box, catch each other's tails, and nip each other's ears. They tumble and scuffle and paw each other's ears gently. As soon as their upper incisors emerge, Chickaree allows them to chew on pieces of nuts and sunflower seeds. But their primary diet is still their mother's milk.

One morning, when the babies are one and a half months old, Chickaree leads them out of the nest and slowly walks ahead of them on the

branch to the tree trunk. The babies are afraid, but their curiosity wins. Wobbly, haltingly, they follow, except one. He refuses to leave the nest and complains softly: kghsee, kghsee, kghsee. The other three reach the tree trunk and hold on fast while Chickaree returns to her timid baby. She nuzzles and licks him, paws him gently and tenderly. This time he follows her. He too is very wobbly. Each time his little body sways to the side, his tail jerks up to keep his balance.

By the time Chickaree has brought him over to the tree trunk, the other three babies are cautiously moving around the tree trunk. Chickaree lets them rest for a while before she teaches them to move head first down the trunk. As they follow their mother slowly and cautiously, their sharp little claws grip the bark tightly. When they reach the lower branch, Chickaree lets them explore the width and density of pine needles while she sits by and keeps an eye on them.

The next day, coming down the tree is
an easy exercise. Now Chickaree brings the
four babies to the very tip of the lower
branch. While they wait to see what hap-
pens next, Chickaree lowers and raises her
head several times, crouches, and jumps.
Then she waits for them in the next tree.
The babies bunch on the tip of the branch
but are afraid to jump. Patiently Chickaree
waits. Finally one baby crouches, lowers and
raises his head exactly as his mother had,

and jumps.

(Chickarees have special eye lenses that enable them to judge distance by raising and lowering their heads.) He almost falls, but grasping the twig end with his paws, he hangs in the air for a few seconds, then quickly scrambles up and runs to his mother. She nuzzles and licks him, and he nestles close to her. When the three remaining babies refuse to jump, Chickaree goes back to encourage them with more nuzzling and licking. When she jumps this time, two babies follow. Now Chickaree sees the insecure baby is still trying to foster his courage to jump.

Suddenly Chickaree screams a warning: chr-r-r-r-r-r, chr-r-r-r-r-r, chr-r-r-r-r-r. A long black snake has appeared at the base of the tree. All the babies except the fourth baby freeze instantly. They flatten their little bodies against the trunk. Chickaree growls at the snake, runs down and stomps her hind feet in anger. The snake stays still. Chickaree flounces her tail vigorously and dashes up and down the tree, but the long black snake does not move.

"Chrghsee, chrghsee, chrghsee," she screams, looking down to see the tip of the black tail disappearing under a brush pile. The danger is past, and Mother Chickaree rushes back to her timid baby, who still moves about the branch, disregarding her warning call.

Each day the chickaree babies become more and more sure of themselves. Each new jump teaches them to judge distances more precisely. Each new run gives them better control of their tails for balance. (They also learn to measure distances from their bodies through the long, sensory hairs called vibrissae located on their cheeks, arms, and sides, under their chins, and at the root of their tails.)

Every day their mother runs faster. She does it on purpose, leaving her babies far behind to figure out the routes for themselves. There are many trees, many branches, and varying distances and heights, and the babies must learn to travel among them quickly and correctly. Their lives will depend on making fast and accurate decisions. The backward baby learns his lessons slowly because he is indecisive. He runs up and down the tree and along every branch to the very tip, but does not know when to jump. He complains constantly: kghsee, kghsee, kghsee. But Mother Chickaree does not run to him any more. She is trying to force him to shift for himself.

Not all the time is spent in learning. On hot summer days Mother Chickaree lets her babies rest and play. But even their games are preparation for their future lives. They box and chase each other and try to catch each other by the rump. When one is caught, he tries to get out of his brother's clutches. He wiggles and tugs, turns and twists, but his brother holds him tight. So both of them topple to the ground and roll and roll—just as they will do in earnest, fighting for their mates or territories when they are grown.

During the play the babies become very hot. Often they flop on the log, open their mouths wide, and pant. They let their feet and tails dangle to cool themselves off as Chickaree

watches for enemies and intruders. Occasionally the babies run up to her to be nuzzled and licked, and to nurse even though they now eat solid food. But they go as quickly as they come, leaving her with the timid baby, who prefers to sit behind his mother and clean her back.

While chasing each other, the baby chickarees also discover new trees, bushes, and birds. They peek into every nook and crevice. They come upon birds' nests full of screaming baby chicks. Protecting his baby chicks, papa blue jay dives at the chickaree babies and drives them away.

Every day around noontime the chickaree babies take a nap. After nursing them Chickaree nuzzles one baby and leads it down under the logs, where she has another escape nest. The baby follows dutifully. Then she comes back up for the second baby, nuzzles it, and takes it below. Soon all four of them are asleep under the log.

While her babies sleep, Mother Chickaree carefully cleans herself, then flops down, exhausted, resting her nose on the log with her feet and tail limply hanging down. But her rest does not last very long. One by one the babies wake up and turn to her to touch noses, huddle close, and nurse, then run off for further play.

The blue jay sees the large hawk first. Y-e-e-e-e-e-ek! Y-e-e-e-e-e-ek! he screams urgently as he dashes into the dense foliage. Birds, gray squirrels, chickarees, and chipmunks run for cover. Chickaree darts to the tree trunk and freezes. Three of her babies also freeze where they are. The timid one runs unheedingly. The hawk plunges, and the cry of the timid baby pierces the silence as the predator bears it away. A few moments later the forest resumes its activity, and bird songs again fill the air. Mother Chickaree sits motionless. Her cheeks quiver and her lower jaw quakes.

But her three remaining babies demand her attention. Now she sees a gray squirrel sneaking up the sweet gum tree, where one baby clings to the trunk still frozen.

Tsuh-tsuh-tsuh-chrrr. Chickaree runs to the tree and stomps her hind feet, moving her torso from side to side. She flounces her tail, chrrrs with each jerk. Wisely the gray squirrel runs past Chickaree's baby and away from Chickaree. Then for the first time the baby stomps its pink feet, flounces its bushy tail, and makes a long, long chr-r-r-r-r. Chickarees have many enemies, most notably the pine marten (from whom they can escape only by falling to the ground), bobcats, fishers, minks, hawks, owls, cats, and snapping turtles that catch chickarees when they swim—and automobiles.

By the middle of June the three babies are completely weaned. From now on they will eat solid food and drink plenty of water every day. Since they are not babies any more, Chickaree chases them away from her more often. It's important that they be on their own, independent, before winter arrives. They must seek out their own food, claim their own territory, and build or find their own nests.

The youngsters have no choice but to venture deeper into the woods. There they meet other chickarees whom they fight for territory. The fight will go on until one of them wins. If the youngster wins, he will get the owner's territory for his own. If not, he will have another fight with another chickaree until he establishes territory of his own. One youngster gets his ear ripped, another his back scratched, the third gets his tail tip-nipped.

It is the end of July. Her youngsters have gone, and Chickaree enjoys being alone again. She eats, naps, cleans, and dusts herself in the sand more leisurely. Bringing up four babies takes time and effort, and Chickaree is tired. The luster of her rusty fur is gone, her white underparts are messy from nursing, and her tail is skinny and shaggy.

In early fall the male chickarees invade the female territory for a second time. Again the woods are full of sqeaks, squeals, chatter, and warning cries. It is not long before Chickaree is pregnant again. She is lucky to be free of her first brood, except for their occasional visits, because some chickarees are pregnant while still weaning their first babies.

Gradually Chickaree's appearance improves. The luster has returned to her rusty coat, and it is molting gradually. Her ear tufts are getting bushier. Like her first brood, who have claimed their territories and are building or fixing their nests, she is hoarding food for winter—nuts, acorns, seeds, dry mushrooms, and the sweet-gum tree cones.

At last the time comes to give birth to her second brood—three tiny, pink babies this time. Now Chickaree's time is divided between taking care of her babies and harvesting more cones. Day and night she nurses them, and the babies grow and grow. Soon their eyes have opened, their steps taken outside the nest, and before the weather becomes cold they are weaned.

Again one youngster is indecisive and slow. It does not participate much in rough tumble-and-tussle play, neither does it join in hide-and-seek or box-and-bite. But it does love boxing while hanging upside down. They have all learned to eat pine seeds, cutting off the tips and scaling the cone. Their mouths are black from pine tree resin. Before they become independent, a pine marten kills the backward youngster. Few chickaree babies survive their first year.

The milkweed cracks and releases its seeds as the wind carries them away to a new beginning. Fewer birds are in the woods; most have

flown south for winter. The berries of the dogwoods are red and ripe now. Chickaree brings
her two youngsters to savor new fruit. In con-
cert with robins and grackles, the chickarees
eat the berries noisily while hanging upside
down! Cottontails, wood sparrows, and cardi-
nals pick up the chips from below.

Chickaree's first youngsters have ended their
visits. They are mature and independent now

and will behave like total strangers whenever they meet—growling, screaming, and fighting each other. Her last two youngsters are fully grown and look exactly like their mother. They will be mature by spring. Now they still frolic and stay near Chickaree. With the winter descending, they do not have time to establish their own territory or build their own nests. They have settled near Chickaree's nest, without much fighting. One made a warm nest in a heap of branches and twigs, the other in a pile of logs, where Chickaree has an escape nest.

Finally the snow falls. All the chickarees have become quieter, less aggressive and noisy. But they remain alert and watchful. No intruder escapes their notice. The youngsters still heed their mother's warning calls.

One extremely cold winter night the two youngsters come to Chickaree's nest. After a few seconds of growling, the three of them huddle close together.

Then another chickaree
comes—a stranger,

and another

and another.

They all growl nervously for a while, but soon they are snuggled tightly together, warming each other with the heat of their bodies, covered with their bushy tails. They may not be related, but they are chickarees struggling to survive. At daybreak they go their separate ways, threatening and growling. Winter will pass. Then, toward the end of February, the woods will come alive again with their screams, chattering, and growls, and the big chase will begin again.

tseew-tseew-tseew   kghsee-kghsee-kghsee

          chr-r-r-r-r-r-rr-r-r-r

gr-r-r-r

          tsee-chrrr-tsee-chrrr-tsee-chrrr

                    tsee-tsee-tsee-chr